Robert Munsch

This book was written with fond memories of my
weekly trips to the Oshawa Public Library
and nightly story-time on the living-room couch.
Thank you, mom and dad, for teaching me to love books.

Frank B. Edwards

Published in Canada by Fitzhenry & Whiteside, 195 Allstate Parkway, Markham, Ontario L3R 4T8
Published in the United States by Fitzhenry & Whiteside, 311 Washington Street, Brighton,
Massachusetts 02135

All inquiries should be addressed to Fitzhenry & Whiteside Limited, 195 Allstate Parkway,
Markham, Ontario L3R 4T8.

www.fitzhenry.ca   godwit@fitzhenry.ca

10 9 8 7 6 5 4 3 2 1

Library and Archives Canada Cataloguing in Publication
Edwards, Frank B., 1952–
Robert Munsch / Frank Edwards.
Includes index.
ISBN 978-1-55455-138-5 (bound). — ISBN 978-1-55455-057-9 (pbk.)
1. Munsch, Robert N., 1945– . 2. Authors, Canadian (English)—20th
century—Biography. 3. Children's literature, Canadian. I. Title.
PS8576.U575Z64 2008   C813'.54   C2008-904614-5

U.S. Publisher Cataloging-in-Publication Data
(Library of Congress Standards)

Edwards, Frank B., 1952–
Robert Munsch / Frank Edwards.
[74] p. : col. photos. ; cm.
Includes index.

Summary: The life and times of Robert Munsch: writer, speaker, father, and Member of the
Order of Canada. His hilarious, often poignant stories have made him one of Canada's
most beloved and best-selling children's authors.
ISBN-978-1-55455-138-5
ISBN- 978-1-55455-057-9 (pbk.)

1. Munsch, Robert N., 1945– —Juvenile literature. 2. Authors, Canadian —20th century
—Biography —Juvenile literature. I. Title.
813.54/22 [B] dc22 PR9199.3.M8667E3 2008

Fitzhenry & Whiteside acknowledges with thanks the Canada Council for the Arts, and the
Ontario Arts Council for their support of our publishing program. We acknowledge the financial
support of the Government of Canada through the Book Publishing Industry Development
Program (BPIDP) for our publishing activities.

Canada Council   Conseil des Arts
for the Arts   du Canada

ONTARIO ARTS COUNCIL
CONSEIL DES ARTS DE L'ONTARIO

Design by Darrell McCalla
Printed in Canada
Cover and back images courtesy of Scholastic Canada Ltd.

Larger
than Life

Robert Munsch

Frank B. Edwards

Fitzhenry & Whiteside

Many thanks to Robert Munsch
for his time and cooperation during the writing of this book,
and for generously supplying photographs and illustrations
from his personal collection.

Contents

The Ordinary Man Next Door

T he life of Robert Munsch, Canada's best known children's author, does not resemble the lives of the people in his crazy, noisy, funny picture books.

Upon ringing the front doorbell of the Munsch family home, a visitor might expect to hear CLOMP CLOMP CLOMP as Robert moves through the hallway and a "YESSSSSS, WHAT DO YOU WAAAAANT!" when he answers the door. But Robert Munsch is different than the crazy adults portrayed in his books. Instead, a pleasant, balding white-haired man comes to the door and says hello in a friendly but shy way. He wears blue jeans, a plaid cotton shirt, and the kind of white running shoes that anyone can buy at Wal-Mart.

With Winston the Yorkshire Terrier in hand, Robert answers the door of his Guelph, Ontario home.

When his two dogs come out to investigate, they don't run through the house knocking over furniture to chase the visitor down the street, barking wildly until the dog catcher and police riot squad show up to rescue him. Instead, they just give a few ordinary woofs as they trot up for a quick sniff and then return to the kitchen when Robert tells them to go lie down.

In spite of selling more than 41 million copies of his books, Robert Munsch doesn't stand out from his neighbors in suburban Guelph, a pleasant university town about an hour's drive west of Toronto. He lives in a neat and tidy house on a quiet, shady street with his wife, Ann Beeler. There probably were some wild and crazy times around the house when the three Munsch kids were little, but they have all grown up and moved away. Most days are pretty quiet now.

Inside, the house walls are painted bright rich colors —deep blue and antique yellow—and the furniture is comfy-cozy. The big family room, with windows looking out over the landscaped back lawn, has a couple of couches but Robert prefers to sit on the floor when he chats to visitors. Or perhaps at the kitchen table.

Even though Robert Munsch is pretty rich and very famous, he seems like a most ordinary kind of guy. When you see him walking down the street, it is easy to forget that he sells about a million books a year and that tens of thousands of kids and parents line up to see the storytelling shows he gives across Canada and the United States.

But as ordinary as he looks, Robert has led a very interesting—occasionally even risky—life that his picture books don't even hint about. From being a weak student in a Catholic school, to a young Jesuit priest-in-training, to an impoverished daycare worker in dangerous slums, Robert Munsch has seen and done things that will never make it into his kids' books.

Chapter One

Growing Up

Young Bobby Munsch with his mother shortly after his first birthday (1946)

Robert Norman Munsch (he doesn't like his middle name) was born on June 11, 1945 in Pittsburgh, Pennsylvania. He grew up in Glenshaw, on the outskirts of Etna, a small steel-mill town in the hills on the northern edge of Pittsburgh. He was the fourth of nine children born to Thomas John Munsch Jr. (1912–2005), a corporate lawyer, and Margaret McKeon (1914–2006). His older siblings were Mary, the eldest, Margie, and

Tommy, who was four years older than Robert. The younger kids were Dickie (born a year after Robert), Billie, Jimmy, Jackie, and Kathy.

Robert was four when his parents bought a large 150-year-old farmhouse set in the middle of a huge yard. Surrounded by fruit trees, it was big enough to hold their growing family and within easy commuting distance to Mr. Munsch's office in Pittsburgh. Mr. Munsch was a smart man who worked as a lawyer for the Philadelphia Company, a large corporation that owned electricity, natural gas, and railroad companies. His own parents, a mining company accountant and a teacher, had filled his childhood home with books, and he passed his passion for reading and stories on to Robert and his other children. Mr. Munsch always warned his children away from "screwdriver work," the kind of manual labor jobs in which he had no interest. While other fathers were handy do-it-yourselfers around the house, Mr. Munsch always hired tradespeople to do household repairs.

Robert's childhood home in Glenshaw, Pennsylvania. At age 14, he inherited his older brother's attic bedroom. There was no heat but plenty of privacy.

Robert's parents, Thomas and Margaret Munsch, pose in their backyard on Mother's Day (1953).

*Dickie, age two, and
Bobby Munsch, age three,
flash mischievous smiles
(1948).*

With three sisters and five brothers, Robert was never short of playmates, although their ages were spread over twenty-five years. In fact, the oldest siblings had graduated from high school and left home by the time the youngest children were born! The Munsch house was a magnet for the neighborhood kids as its big backyard boasted a sandbox, a baseball diamond, and a huge sycamore tree with a swing. There were apple, pear, peach, and butternut trees to climb and an old shed that served as a playhouse. On weekends and over the summer holidays, children would drop by to play with whoever was outside in the yard. Their adventures took them into the woods that covered the hillside and to a nearby creek. Robert was a passionate tree-climber, dam-builder, and stick-floater.

Dressed for cold weather, Bobby Munsch poses in front of the family home about 1948.

The road that ran in front of the house was too steep for safe cycling so Robert never had a bicycle, but the library and Pearce's Drugstore were easy destinations for walking. By the time he was seven or eight, Robert was allowed to wander the neighborhood with his friends. Sometimes, his mother would give him money if he wanted to visit Pearce's soda fountain for an ice cream soda, a Coke float, or some penny candy. By the time he was 10, Robert was a regular visitor to Etna's public library, reading about two books a day during the summer months. By grade five, Robert was reading 200 books a year.

Thomas' Snowsuit

While Robert had to wear snowsuits as a kid, he got the idea for *Thomas' Snowsuit* during a performance in Halifax. The audience consisted of 300 preschoolers who were all wearing snowsuits. After Robert had told all his regular stories, he made one up on the spot about a little boy who hated wearing his snowsuit to school.

In the story, a kindergartener refuses to put on his snowsuit for his teacher. By the time the principal joins in the struggle, Thomas is in his underwear, the principal is wearing a dress, and the teacher is wearing the principal's suit.

Thomas' Snowsuit

Robert Munsch   Michael Martchenko

Robert holds a bouquet of tree blossoms while posing with three of his brothers. Big brother Tom holds onto Billie. Dickie is on the left.

As he got older, his chores included burning trash in a barrel behind the house and, when there were no adult eyes watching, Robert, his younger brother Dickie, and their friends would make fireballs out of burning crayons and plastic. Such unauthorized burning ended on the day that little David Seal got struck on the head with a burning piece of plastic. He ran screaming in panic around the yard, with kids and Mr. Munsch chasing after him as they tried to remove the smoldering blob from his head. As usual when a kid got injured in the neighborhood, David was taken across the road to Dr. Wallace who performed "battle surgery" on all the kids who showed up with cuts, burns, and broken limbs.

Robert Munsch

The Munsch parents were devout Roman Catholics who raised their children to respect and honor the Church. While his older brother, Tommy, didn't like to follow rules and was often in trouble for misbehaving at school and in the neighborhood, young Robert had no trouble obeying his parents and paid close attention to his religious instructors.

Sunday was always an important day of the week that started with a huge family breakfast followed by a trip to "the big, enormous German Catholic Church" in Etna. Before putting on their best clothes, the older children would take turns preparing platters of eggs, bacon, ham, cornbread, pancakes, and waffles, trying to outdo the previous Sunday's breakfast. Then, after getting dressed, they would pile into the large Munsch family station wagon for the drive to church where incense, Latin chants, organ music, and messages of thrift and hard work awaited them. Later, with the priests' voices still ringing in their ears, the Munsch kids would file down the steps of the church and head back to their crowded car, ready for the drive  to their grandmother's house for a large Sunday dinner.

Saturday nights were also special. Mr. Munsch bought one of the first televisions in the neighborhood and the entire family would gather around it on Saturdays to watch shows about the old American west, filled with good guys and bad guys and people who needed help from heroes like *Gunsmoke's* Marshal Matt Dillon and gentleman-gunfighter "Paladin" on *Have Gun, Will Travel*. One of Robert's favorite shows was *Howdy Doody*, one of America's first children's television shows, which featured Buffalo Bob and his puppet friend Howdy.

Sleeping arrangements at the Munsch house were based on age. When he was little, Robert shared a bedroom with his younger brothers who were known as the "little boys." At age eight, he and his younger brother Dickie, who was seven, graduated to a small room with one big bed—a sure sign they were growing up. Robert finally got his own bed when he was 14 since his older brother, Tommy, had moved away to college. Tommy's old third-storey attic room had no heat and no insulation, making it hot in the summer and cold in the winter, but Robert was happy to have his very own bedroom. It gave him the privacy that he wanted when it was time to read.

And Robert read a lot. There was a set of *National Geographic* magazines dating back to 1902 in the attic. Robert read them one at a time, becoming a junior expert at everything from African tribes to nuclear technology. When he was young, he loved Dr. Seuss stories (his favorite was *The 500 Hats of Bartholomew Cubbins*) and was certain that the little Scottish terrier in Marjorie Flack's picture book, *Angus Lost,* was the same Angus that lived next door to him. (He wasn't.) But by the time Robert was 10, he had grown interested in non-fiction, and his favorite author became Isaac Asimov, a famous science-fiction writer.

The Munsch house was filled with hundreds of books. All the children were voracious readers who were encouraged to share their ideas with the rest of the family, especially around the dining table. Meal times might not have been fancy—Mrs. Munsch was a meat, potatoes, and boiled vegetable kind of cook—but it didn't matter because conversation was usually the main course. Older brother Tommy would sometimes get into such complicated discussions with Mr. Munsch about science and arithmetic that they would abandon their plates of pork and sauerkraut and move to the kitchen to work out a mathematical formula on the big blackboard that was supposed to be used for family messages.

Mr. Munsch also loved to tell bedtime stories to his children and he had such a good imagination that he seldom relied on books. All the youngsters would gather in the "little boys'" room and get swept into very long stories that would sometimes go on for weeks at a time. Their father loved to do different voices for all his characters, complete with exaggerated accents and improvised sound effects. Each night he would pick up where he had left off and give his children another chapter in the long stories he made up on the spot.

The Munsch house at 1210 Mount Royal Boulevard was a happy and active place to grow up and Robert loved living there. But in 1951, when he was six, it was time to start school—and that was a place that made young Robert very unhappy.

Chapter Two

School Days

O n the first day of school, Mr. Munsch drove Robert to All Saints School on Davey Street in the big family station wagon and took him to meet his teacher and classmates. It was not a happy time for Robert: The class was crowded with sixty other grade one students and the nuns who ran the school were very strict. Students were expected to sit quietly at their desks, face forward, and put all thoughts of play out of their minds.

At about age eight, Robert got dressed up for his first communion at the Roman Catholic Church in Etna, Pennsylvania.

Compared to the easy-spirited house full of books and family that he left behind each day, the school was like a prison with its crowded classrooms and hallways. Robert, who preferred books to people, didn't like it at all. One of the reasons the school was so crowded was due to the "baby boom" that occurred after the Second World War. A population explosion had begun in the United States (and Canada) when hundreds of thousands of soldiers returned home from the war, anxious to get married and start families. So many babies were born that schools were crammed full until new schools could be built.

To make matters worse, Robert was a daydreamer who did not do well in class, even though he was well-behaved. He was easily bored and found it difficult to pay attention. Often, Robert left his homework assignments uncompleted.

Today, Robert remembers his early school days sadly. "It was a very crowded school. A very structured school. You had to memorize stuff…it was very challenging. I couldn't spell and I couldn't do math so it was very challenging for me. Let's say it didn't use my strong points."

School was hard for him: kids called him "Dumb Bobby," his report cards were filled with comments about his poor work habits, and his grades were usually low. At family gatherings, the adults would shake their heads and look sad when they talked about "poor Bobby." Mr. Munsch was worried that he would be stuck doing "screwdriver work" while his siblings became lawyers and engineers. When teachers considered failing Robert, they were reminded that his brother, Dickie, was just a year behind and so Robert was always promoted to the next grade to be saved from the humiliation of being passed by his younger brother.

As Robert sums it up, "I never learned how to spell, graduated from eighth grade counting on my fingers to do simple addition and, in general, was not a resounding academic success."

What Robert and his parents didn't realize at the time, however, was that the school system itself was largely to blame for Robert's lack of academic success. At that time, students at the school learned to read from textbooks and "readers." They didn't have to complete novel studies or book reports until grade eight, which meant that Robert was not getting any credit for being a reading genius, even though he was reading about four books a week—much of it adult non-fiction. His teachers were so busy paying attention to what he wasn't doing well, they didn't recognize his special talents. Even worse, there was no creative writing taught, so his artistic talents were also being ignored. Eventually, little "Bobby's" love of books

Robert

A class picture shows Robert at All Saints School, second from the right in the fourth row.

saved his shaky academic career—but not until most of his teachers had labeled him a failure.

It was his love of books that brought him into contact with Sister Emma Jean Middendorf, a young nun who was the school librarian when Robert was in grade four. Even though students didn't have to read extra books for school, the young librarian tried to interest the students in books for fun and was delighted by Robert's enthusiasm for her library. Although Robert had a reputation as a poor student, Sister Emma Jean quickly learned about his voracious appetite for books. She decided that he was actually a very intelligent boy who simply didn't do well at the subjects his teachers were interested in. Knowing that his parents were worried about him, she sent them a note assuring them that Robert was actually quite smart and would possibly grow up to be an artist of some kind.

Sister Emma Jean also had enough of a sense of humor to appreciate Robert's quirky view of life and, when he brought a sign for her office one day, she thanked him and hung it above her desk. It said:"You don't have to be crazy to work here but it helps." By that time, Robert was working with Sister Emma Jean in the library as a volunteer helper. In 1958, when All Saints School was being expanded, Sister Emma Jean had been given the task of creating a brand new library. When 13-year-old Robert saw her typing out cata- logue cards for each book in the library, he offered to help—working with her after school and on Saturdays, even over the summer. They became good friends and still keep in touch with each other today.

By the time he left elementary school, Robert had finally established himself as a kid who was smart at some things—especially topics that had been covered by *National Geographic*—although he had also become a loner who found it hard to form friendships. To make things worse, he began to suffer from bouts of depression. Clouds of gloom would descend on him, making him feel sad and isolated.

"I didn't know what was the matter," he now says. "It was just wrecking my life. It was making me socially non-functional—a wacko."

Convinced that he would never fit in with the world around him, he decided to become a Roman Catholic priest when he grew up. Until then, however, he had to survive four years of high school.

Robert does not have fond memories of his high school years. He wasn't popular, didn't play sports, and only dated girls in his final year. Although his marks improved as he became more interested in his courses, he remained a loner. The only club he joined was the biology club where he learned about animals and insects, and occasionally got to dissect them. A self-described nerd, he even refused to cheer at the school's football and basketball games he attended. He was a very unhappy young man whose sole pleasure seemed to come from the books that he read constantly, usually in the privacy of his attic bedroom.

His quiet, isolated life seemed like perfect preparation for the priesthood and he was relieved when he finally graduated from North Catholic High School in 1963.

Chapter Three

Life as a Jesuit

In 1963, Robert entered a Jesuit novitiate where he and his fellow novices wore simple cassocks to show their disinterest in worldly fashion.

In the summer of 1963, most teenagers in Pittsburgh were listening to Porky Chedwick's rock-and-roll show on WAMO radio and dancing to the music of a new band from England called The Beatles. But that music was not a part of Robert Munsch's life for the next four years as he withdrew from the ordinary world of American teenagers to start his training as a priest. Instead of t-shirts and tight jeans, Robert wore a plain dark cassock—a rough, woolen robe like the one worn by Friar Tuck in the Robin Hood movies.

Robert and his friend, John Maloney, graduated from high school in 1963.

While his fellow high school graduates were starting college, 17-year-old Robert entered a very different kind of educational life at a Jesuit novitiate in Wernersville, Pennsylvania. Set far from the distractions of the outside world in an area known for its rolling countryside and health resorts, the novitiate was a cloistered Catholic school that held 180 young men who had all taken a vow of poverty, chastity, and obedience to God. Serving as novices, they learned what it takes to become a member of the Order

Best Friends

What do a world-famous storytelling children's author and a California-based computer expert have in common? They were best friends in high school in Etna, Pennsylvania. While Robert was a loner most of the time, preferring books to people, he did have one close buddy—John Maloney who now lives in San Jose. Aside from a love of science, they had another important thing in common. Both of them had eight brothers and sisters.

of Jesus while living completely separate from the rest of the world. Robert had decided in grade eight that he wanted to become a priest, and he was finally getting a chance to work toward that goal.

The life of a young novice was not easy. A novitiate functions like an army boot camp where new recruits must give up their individual identity to become soldiers who think and act alike. At Wernersville, Robert and his fellow religious novices were not allowed to own anything personal except for a few books. They all dressed alike in their medieval cassocks and were told how to act and talk, and even how to think. Everything they did and said was open to criticism by their Jesuit leaders and fellow students.

Although he had his own bedroom in the novices' dormitory, Robert had little privacy—none of the rooms had doors on them. To make sure that no one became too comfortable in one place, the novices had to switch rooms every month.

Each long day was filled with prayers and religious instruction, much of it in Latin, an ancient language that Robert did not know well. The novices' days were carefully scheduled from

The Jesuits

Jesuits are members of the Order of Jesus, the Catholic Church's largest religious order. More than 18,000 Jesuits, spread through more than 100 countries, have dedicated themselves to caring for others. These men are well known for their missionary work and teaching—the Jesuits operate schools, colleges, and universities around the world, including Georgetown University in Washington and Fordham University in New York. They also have a reputation for fighting for the rights of oppressed people even when it brings them into conflict with governments.

The Order of Jesus was founded by a Spanish student, Ignatius of Loyola, and his six friends who were studying together in Paris in 1534. They created vows of chastity, poverty, and obedience to the Church that are still followed by today's Jesuits.

dawn to dark and they had no free time of their own. The only opportunities that he had to escape from the dull routines of the novitiate came when he made trips to local communities to work with people in need of help.

While he had escaped the teenage world of sports and dating, Robert was not fully convinced that this was the type of quiet life he really wanted. When he emerged from the novitiate in 1966, he had been out of touch with youth culture for four years and was surprised by the changes that America had undergone. Music, fashion, and society had been turned upside down. Love beads, peace signs, and hippies with long hair were everywhere.

"What happened to people's hair?" he asked. "What are all those weird clothes?"

Much of the change had been inspired by protests against a war that he knew little about. The United States was drafting tens of thousands of young men Robert's age into the army and sending them to fight in Vietnam. While college students across the country were demonstrating for peace and protesting against all kinds of authority—against the government and church and parents—Robert had been busy studying and obeying the Jesuits' rules.

After he graduated from the cloistered life of Wernersville, the Jesuits sent Robert to its seminary on Fordham University's campus in Shrub Oaks, New York to study history and philosophy. Since he found these courses very interesting, he studied them enthusiastically. Along with volunteer work, the Jesuits are known for their high academic standards in a variety of subjects like science, mathematics, and the arts. Robert was expected to do well in school and perform community service work at the same time. He did both. In the summer of 1968, he got a break from seminary life by volunteering to spend a summer in Baltimore, Maryland, helping prepare lower-income African-American students for high school by improving their reading skills.

Having grown up as a bookworm, Robert was a keen literacy teacher and found his volunteer work with young teenagers interesting and rewarding. While the tutoring was a welcome escape from his academic life, it also gave him his first encounter with life in the slums and the problems faced by minorities in America's big cities. While at times he might have been unsure about being a Jesuit, Robert definitely liked helping children improve their lives.

Although he enjoyed university life more than the novitiate, it was his weekend work during the school year as a recreation volunteer at St. Joseph's orphanage in Peekskill, New York that was really going to affect his life. Every Saturday, he spent a few hours with the thirty girls of Group 2 who were all below the age of fourteen. Under the stern eye of a nun, he played games with them—and told them stories.

"I first started telling stories in the orphanage because of my father," he recalls. "At the time, I didn't place great value on it. It was just something you did. It was nothing special at all. Some people made play dough. Some people made up stories."

Most of the 650 children at the orphanage were African-American or Puerto Rican, and had been plucked from New York City. They had little chance of ever being adopted and feeling the love of a family as Robert had. The nuns were strict with the children, even harsh at times, and he was shocked to learn that they would iron the girls'

During his years studying at Fordham University, Robert would visit the young residents of St. Joseph's Orphanage in Peekskill, New York (circa 1966).

curly hair in the belief that straight hair was healthier. He felt sorry for the girls and made up funny stories to make them laugh.

Although his stories were popular, some of his popularity also came from the fact that he was one of the only males that the girls got to meet. For that reason especially, "Brother Bob" was a valued visitor.

After finishing his studies in New York, Robert moved to Cambridge, Massachusetts, near Boston, to study anthropology, which is the study of human societies around the world. His plan was to earn a doctorate; then the Jesuits would decide whether he would become a missionary in Africa or Central America, or become a university professor.

But that plan changed in the autumn of 1971 at the end of a day of volunteer work at a Boston daycare center. After getting off the subway in the rough neighborhood where he lived with a houseful of other Jesuits, Robert was dragged into an alley and beaten so badly that his attacker left him for dead. Despite serious head wounds and other injuries, Robert managed to drag himself down the street to get help. After many months of recovery, Robert discovered that his injuries had seriously affected his memory.

"I lost parts of my life," he explains by comparing his brain to a computer. "Parts of the disk were gone and they never came back. I didn't realize that until I went back home and was talking to my family. It was like they were reading a different book that had more chapters than mine."

He had been working on a Ph.D. and doing well in school but his brain injuries affected his studies. A few months after the attack, he failed the university exams that would have made him a Doctor of Anthropology. He decided to quit the Jesuits and reconsider his future.

To help clear his mind, he took a long vacation with his younger brother, Dickie, who had just gotten out of the army after fighting in Vietnam. Both brothers needed time to think about their lives so they loaded up Dick's old white Volkswagen Beetle and spent the summer of 1972 camping, driving first to Seattle, Washington and then south to the Grand Canyon in Arizona. Sitting around campfires with his brother talking about their lives each night, Robert decided that he liked working with children more than anything else he had done. His mind was made up. He was going to return to Boston, not as a priest or a student, but as a daycare worker where he could help people improve their lives. He was going to change the world, one child at a time.

Chapter Four

Daycare Days

H aving once taken a vow of poverty, Robert adapted readily enough to a life where good works were more important than a high-paying job. But, of course, once he left the world of the Jesuits, he had to earn enough money to feed and clothe himself. He moved into a rundown apartment in Boston's rough Jamaica Plain district and found his first job as a daycare worker. Boston University had established an experimental cooperative daycare to explore the benefits of early education on preschool children. Work at the university's Bromely Heath Infant Daycare was shared by paid staff like Robert and the mothers of the children who attended.

Sweeping up glass, a daily chore at Bromely Heath Infant Daycare, Jamaica Plains, Boston, Massachusetts (1972)

Jamaica Plain was not an easy place for kids to grow up. Drugs and crime were everywhere. The children in the daycare center were poor and usually African-American. They lived in a rundown public housing project, and their mothers were uneducated single parents. Boston University hoped that this experimental daycare center would help the mothers in two ways: By learning how to run their own daycare center they would gain important job skills; and they would also be doing something that would help them look after and raise their children.

Of course, Robert was not a childcare expert himself, although he had plenty of experience with kids; not only did he come from a large family, but he had also spent many hours as a Jesuit volunteer at St. Joseph's Orphanage and the Cambridge daycare. Each day he went to work tackling all kinds of jobs, from fixing meals and changing diapers to leading games and supervising nap time. He still suffered from regular periods of depression, but he also experienced days when he was super-happy and energetic—a perfect mood for entertaining young kids. While other workers might scold children who didn't lie quietly during naptime, Robert would keep them quiet by telling stories, complete with funny sound effects, just like his father had done back in Etna.

Despite his white, middle-class background, Robert was popular with the children and their mothers. "It was wonderful," he says. "The daycare staff decided I was really great with kids and [those families] were some of the most wonderful people I will ever know." Most of the women had come to Boston from the American Deep South as children themselves, and while their lives in Jamaica Plain were hard, they felt that their own young kids had better opportunities for a good education there than back in the South.

Suddenly that year, Robert's life began to make sense. If he had not studied to become a Jesuit, he never would have discovered the inner city problems of North America. Today, he reflects, "I would have been a nice suburban kid who didn't understand poor America."

Not only did Robert love his job and newfound freedom, he also fell in love for the first time. One day in the fall of 1972, he met university student Ann Beeler while changing a baby's very stinky diaper and quickly fell in love with her. Ann, who had grown up in Rochester, New York, was finishing a degree in child studies at Tufts University and doing a work placement at the daycare. One of their first dates was dinner at Robert's slum apartment. After finishing a pot of tea, they found two dead cockroaches at the bottom of the teapot. Robert was frantic with apologies but Ann thought it was funny and laughed.

In January 1973, Robert and Ann were married, drawn together by love and a desire to make the lives of children better. When Ann graduated, she took over Robert's full-time

The newlyweds, Robert and Ann (1973)

job at the daycare center so that he could take the same child studies course at Tufts University that she had just completed. As much as they liked living in Boston, Ann and Robert realized that they needed to move to a safer neighborhood. One day, Ann was assaulted on the street and had to run into busy traffic to escape her attackers. Soon after, Robert got into trouble with a street gang after he reported some members to the police for stealing a car. When the gang vowed revenge, the daycare mothers encouraged Robert and Ann to leave the city for their own safety.

In 1974, Robert once again found himself driving across America, this time in a white Volkswagen station wagon with his wife. They traveled until their money ran out and then began to look for work in Oregon. Ann was hired at a daycare center in Coos Bay, a busy lumber town located beside the Pacific Ocean, and Robert was hired a short time later. The pace of life was slower and less dangerous than in Boston. Living close to the ocean, they could take long walks on rainforest trails and across the sand dunes along the shore. At night, they listened to foghorns and the noises of ships in the harbor, and smelled the scent of fresh-cut cedar drifting in from a local mill.

Life in Coos Bay was very different from Jamaica Plains. It was a safer, more pleasant community for children and daycare workers—an easier place to live even if the couple wasn't earning much money. They enjoyed their jobs and Robert began to take his storytelling sessions more seriously. Each day he would invent a new story for the children, just as his father had done for the Munsch children at bedtime for so many years. But he soon discovered that some of his stories were more popular than others and that the kids wanted to hear the best ones over and over again. One of their favorites was about a princess and a dragon—several years later, it would become famous as *The Paper Bag Princess*.

But, of course, all good things must eventually come to an end. After two years in Coos Bay, Robert and Ann were laid off when the state government reduced the amount of money it gave to daycare centers. Since they needed to find new jobs, it was time to hit the road again.

Robert and Ann celebrating their second anniversary at the Coos Bay, Oregon daycare (1975)

Climbing back into their old Volkswagen, the couple drove east. They were convinced that their careers would always involve children, but they were unsure about returning to a large American city. They visited several cities but were always discouraged by the stories of racism and violence they heard. Finally, they decided to drive to Toronto to visit a friend in 1975. They had never been to Canada before but were impressed immediately by the people and places they saw.

Robert remembers asking, "Where are the boarded-up buildings?" As they drove through the inner city neigh-borhoods of Toronto, they didn't feel scared. The city seemed safer and friendlier than Boston and they decided to stay.

A friend told them about a daycare job that had suddenly become available at the University of Guelph, about an hour's drive west of Toronto. Robert applied and was immediately hired to teach a university course in child studies and to run the depart-ment's daycare program each morning. Later, Ann was offered a similar job at the daycare and the couple was told they could

A freshly shaved Robert poses with Ann the day before his daycare job interview in Guelph (1975)

remain in Canada permanently if they wanted to settle down. Their answer was, yes!

Chapter Five

A Storytale Job

University of Guelph

Guelph was certainly different from inner-city Boston. Founded in 1827 by Scottish settlers, it was a small city of less than 75,000 people when the Munsches arrived in 1975. Many of its old downtown buildings had been carefully restored, and its older neighborhoods consisted of brick homes with front porches along tree-lined streets. It was a safe and affordable city—a good place for a young couple who hoped to have a house of their own and fill it with children.

The University of Guelph is one of Canada's oldest universities and, Robert discovered, a beautiful place to work. Its campus resembles a big park with sprawling lawns and large shady trees. The university itself is made up of a mix of old and new buildings, a few of which are barns filled with animals belonging to the veterinary and agricultural colleges. Each morning, Robert would wander across the grounds to the department of Family Studies where he managed its "laboratory" preschool. All morning, he would supervise the daycare staff and the university students who were learning to be childcare workers. In the afternoons, he would bid the preschoolers goodbye and head upstairs to a classroom to deliver a lecture to his much older university students.

The preschool was considered a laboratory because Family Studies students spent time there getting practical experience as part of their program. While working with the children, they could try out the lessons on child behavior they had been studying in class. In addition, they would sometimes slip into a room beside the daycare that had a large one-way mirror that allowed students and professors to observe the activities of the preschoolers. It was that one-way mirror that eventually established Robert Munsch's reputation as the most entertaining storyteller on campus.

Robert's favorite daycare activity was story time when he could sit down with the kids and tell them stories as he had been doing before in Coos Bay and Boston. But this time, there were adults watching quietly behind the mirror, trying not to laugh as Robert made funny faces and hilarious noises. One of those adults was Robert's boss, Dr. Bruce Ryan, whose wife, Nancy, was a children's librarian. They were both impressed by his wild stories and their popularity with the children. Sometimes Robert would try out a new story and other times the children would insist that he retell one of his older pieces. Whenever he retold a story, he made it a little bit better, changing characters and details until he thought it was just right.

Ann also worked at the preschool and occasionally heard the stories, too. After listening to one of Robert's favorites about a prince named Ronald rescuing a princess who had been kidnapped by a dragon, Ann suggested that the idea of the brave prince was too old fashioned. Why not have the princess rescue the prince, she suggested. Robert liked the idea and one of his most famous stories, *The Paper Bag Princess*, was born. He named the princess Elizabeth after a four-year old who attended the preschool because he thought that she was a bit spoiled and acted like a princess at times. The kids who had heard the story before didn't seem to notice the change but their mothers certainly did. They liked the idea of Elizabeth NOT need-ing a prince to solve her problem. In fact, they loved the ending when the princess calls Ronald a bum after he complains that she is messy and badly dressed after the rescue. Almost by accident, Robert's funny story had become a powerful feminist lesson.

Meanwhile, Bruce and Nancy Ryan were convinced that Robert's stories would make great picture books. Robert had never thought of becoming an author before, and he wasn't very interested in writing his stories down until Dr. Ryan gave him a two-month "research break" (with full pay) in 1978 on the condition that he prepare 10 of his stories for publication. For the first few weeks, Robert just fooled around, enjoying his unexpected holiday. Then, at the end of the break, he had to rush to get 10 stories written down on paper and mail them to 10 different publishers. He knew nothing about being an author and did not pick the publishers very carefully. Some were so small that they eventually went out of business. Others were so big that they didn't pay much attention to an author no one knew. In the end, just one publisher liked his stories.

Annick Press was a small Toronto company that had just been in business for three years and had only published six books. But its owners, Rick Wilkes and Anne Millyard, really liked the stories. They thought that they sounded especially good when read aloud—a result of Robert's constant revisions.

Getting Published

• Write a story. Read it out loud to learn what it sounds like. Keep rewriting it until it sounds great.

• Show your story to family and friends and ask for suggestions that make it even better.

• Research different publishing companies and find ones that publish the sort of story you have written.

• Find their submissions guidelines on their websites and read their rules carefully. Make sure that you follow their instructions.

• Once you have sent in your story, be prepared to WAIT for several weeks or months for a response. Write them a polite "reminder" letter if you haven't heard back after two months.

• If your story is accepted, CONGRATULATIONS! Thousands of stories are submitted to publishers every year, but only a fraction of them are published. The editor may want changes to make the story better.

• If your story is rejected, think about any comments that the publisher might have sent to you. Consider reworking your story.

• Send your story to another publisher. Many famous authors have had good stories rejected dozens of times.

• Start work on your next story.

Annick Press immediately agreed to publish two of his books in 1979. The first was *Mud Puddle* about a girl named Jule Ann who gets ambushed by mud puddles falling out of trees whenever she goes outside wearing clean clothes. The story had been inspired by the preschoolers in Guelph who were always getting muddy when they played out-side after a rainstorm. The main character was named after one of Robert's favorite daycare kids and the story was one of his most requested. Robert claims to have told it every day for almost two months.

Annick's second Munsch book that year was *The Dark*, which was also about Jule Ann. Instead of battling mud puddles, she was dealing with darkness that leapt out of a cookie jar and grew ever bigger and more menacing as it swallowed up all the shadows in the house. The first two books were illustrated by a Finnish-Canadian artist named Sami Suomalainen, an artist who was almost as new to publishing as Robert was.

For its third book, Annick selected one of Robert's favorites—*The Paper Bag Princess*—but it wanted a different style of artwork, so Rick, Anne, and Robert went looking for a new illustrator. While attending a graphic arts show in Toronto, they came across a picture of gulls with airplane landing-gear instead of feet and agreed that it must have come from an artist with a suitably wild imagination. They were right. Michael Martchenko was a forty-year-old Toronto advertising illustrator and art director with a wacky sense of humor who had been drawing since he was a child in France.

Working with Robert

Illustrator Michael Martchenko has worked with Robert Munsch since 1980, when he brought a fiesty little princess and her selfish prince to life in *The Paper Bag Princess* with his playful watercolor pictures. In their early days together, Michael found Robert to be a shy man who expressed his opinions quietly during their editorial meetings. Then he attended his first Munsch performance. He thought his friend was going to just read some stories to children. "It was a big surprise," he says. "Bob was on stage making funny noises and crazy faces and the kids went wild."

After reading *The Paper Bag Princess*, Michael did some rough sketches and a storyboard that showed how the story could be told in pictures. Robert and Annick liked his work and his enthusiasm, so they hired him to create the illustrations for the book that would turn into Robert Munsch's first bestseller.

When it was published in 1980, *The Paper Bag Princess* sold 3,000 copies, making it Annick's most successful book to date. Even more copies sold the following year. Book reviewers and teachers alike loved the strong female character and the surprising twist at the end of the story. Suddenly, it seemed that lots of people in Canada wanted more Robert Munsch stories—especially teachers, librarians, and the editors at Annick, who had gone back to the small pile of Munsch manuscripts still on their desks in search of their next title.

Amazingly, the book which started out as a story-time tale in Coos Bay, went on to become one of Robert Munsch's most popular books. More than three million copies have been sold since it was first published. It has been turned into an animated video and translated into dozens of languages. There is even a Paper Bag Princess doll!

The Paper Bag Princess
Story • Robert N. Munsch Art • Michael Martchenko

Of course, selling a few thousand copies of a book doesn't really make an author financially successful but, in 1985, Robert decided to quit his job anyway so that he could concentrate on storytelling as a full-time job. He was quite happy making up stories and sharing them with children, although at first he had trouble finding schools that would invite him to visit. That began to change as more of his books were published. And, at the insistence of Rick Wilkes and Anne Millyard at Annick, Robert began to write his most popular stories down, putting them in a folder where he could work on them a little bit each week—tweaking and rewriting them until they were ready to be turned into books.

There might not have been a lot of money to be earned as a full-time storyteller but Robert and Ann had survived on low-paying jobs before and they planned to do it again, by living in a small townhouse and shopping carefully. Compared to the rough days in Boston, their lives in Canada seemed pretty good.

Chapter Six

Love You Forever

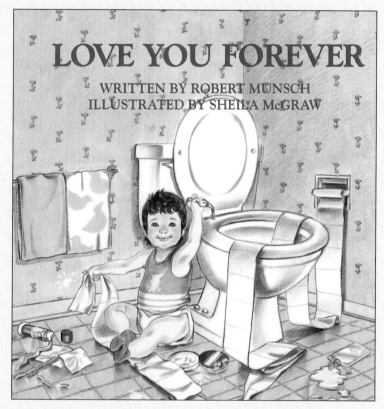

LOVE YOU FOREVER

WRITTEN BY ROBERT MUNSCH
ILLUSTRATED BY SHEILA McGRAW

Well before Annick had published his first books, life in Guelph seemed to be going pretty well for Robert and Ann. They had good jobs, good friends, and they had each other. Even Robert's depression was finally under control. A doctor had given him medicine to stabilize his moods—instead of feeling awful some days and crazy-happy on others, now he just felt normal most of the time.

With everything going so well, they decided that it was time to start a family. But both times that Ann became pregnant, the babies died before they could be born. After so many years of devoting their lives to other people's children, Robert and Ann were devastated to learn from the doctors that they would not be able to have children of their own. One day when he was feeling sad, Robert made up a song for his little unborn babies.

I'll love you forever
I'll like you for always,
As long as I'm living
my baby you'll be.

It was a sad but peaceful song to comfort his emptiness and was never meant to become a story or a book. But one day, at a storytelling session in a large auditorium at the university in 1980, Robert began to think of a story to go with the song, a story about a mother who watches her baby grow up and never stops loving him. Even as the baby grows up and does all sorts of bad things like flushing a watch down the toilet, the mother still sings her song to the boy, continuing to rock him in her arms even after he grows up. The story ends with her adult son, rocking his old, old mother in his arms singing the lullaby to her.

Every now and then, an author miraculously has a story form in his brain almost instantly. This sort of miracle happened to Robert while he was on stage that day in Guelph. His sad song inspired an instant story. As he was talking to the audience, he just made it up on the spot and the story received some very interesting reactions.

The kids loved it and thought it was very funny, laughing at the idea of a mother singing to a teenager, and an adult son rocking his old mother. And the adults in the room loved it too but for a very different reason. They felt its sadness and understood its message about the love of a parent for a child. Robert began to tell it at every story-telling session and the more he recited it, the more people told him to turn it into a book.

But when Robert took it to Annick, the publishers said that they couldn't publish it because it wasn't a children's book. They said it was a parents' book. Instead, they sent him to another company, Firefly Books, which agreed to publish it. Sheila McGraw, an illustrator with no experience in children's books, was hired to do the pictures. *Love You Forever* was finally released in 1986—the same year that Robert became a Canadian citizen.

At first things did not look good. Most book reviewers disliked the story and they all seemed to hate the old-fashioned pictures in it. One reviewer wrote, "This is not a children's story." Another wrote, "This is sentimentality at its worst." Both agreed that "Munsch should go back to what he does best."

But the mothers and grandmothers who shop at book-stores must have loved it because it sold 30,000 copies in its first year and 70,000 in the year after that. Robert recalls the new publisher telling him not to get too excited—not to expect it to last. "It didn't," he laughs. "In 1988, it sold one million [copies] and has been selling about a million copies a year ever since. I think the book works because it lets people think about what life is all about."

Suddenly, after publishing sixteen books, Robert Munsch had become really famous. Everyone seemed to be talking about *Love You Forever*. Not surprisingly, it is still one of Robert's favorite stories because it is a memorial to his and Ann's lost babies.

언제까지나 너를 사랑해

Love You Forever

글 · 로버트 먼치 그림 · 안토니 루이스 옮김 · 김숙

Munsch Around the World

When a book is really successful in North America, foreign publishers will often buy the rights to publish it in their own countries. So far Munsch books have been translated into more than 20 languages. But sometimes the text stays the same and the artwork changes.

A few years after it brought the original *Love You Forever* to the United Kingdom, editors at Random House decided to try a version with funnier pictures. Anthony Lewis's illustrations are more cartoonish than Sheila McGraw's original work and became more popular with British readers. Publishers in Korea, Norway, and Sweden use the same artwork.

With more than 25 million copies in print, it is also probably the bestselling book ever written by a Canadian author. In fact, it ranks among the bestselling children's books in the world, although it follows far behind J.K. Rowling's *The Philosopher's Stone* which has sold 107 million copies. Sales of *Love You Forever* continue to stand at about a million copies a year and Robert's royalties have allowed him the financial freedom to do anything he wants. Like visit schools all across North America to tell stories to children—for free!

Chapter Seven

Robert Munsch Comes to Town

To many people's surprise, Robert does not consider himself an author. Even though the books he has written have earned him millions of dollars and made him famous, Robert Munsch believes that he is a storyteller first and an author second. Of course, he really does tell stories well—to the delight of children, he uses his whole body to deliver a story. His voice makes funny noises, his eyes go screwy, and he distorts his face and waves his arms around as he prances around an audience, acting out his characters. Sometimes he even changes the words when he thinks of a better line or a different name. These are all things that printed books cannot do—the pictures and words stay the same every time a reader turns a page. Nothing changes.

While most authors sit down at a typewriter or computer to create their stories at a desk, Robert takes a different approach. After he gets an idea and makes up a story, he usually doesn't write it down. Instead, he keeps it in his head, shaping it and thinking about it until he is ready to share it with an audience of kids. Sometimes, those early performances are fantastic but often they are not—Robert relies on the reaction of his audience to tell him how good or bad a story really is. If he is interested in the story, he tells it again and again, changing it over and over until he thinks it is finally finished. Then he types it up, adding it to the 200 unpublished stories he keeps on his computer.

He takes his job as a storyteller very seriously. In the early days when he had a few stories ready to try out —either because they were new or had been rewritten— he would share them with his preschoolers at the university. But he quit that job in 1985, so now he has to find new audiences for his storytelling experiments.

"When I started out," he recalls today, "I couldn't pay people to let me come and tell stories.… I'd ask, 'Can I come and tell stories at the school? NO!!!' "But when word finally got out about how much children loved to hear his stories, suddenly hundreds of teachers wanted him to visit. "Now," says Robert, "I can get into any school or any situation I want."

These days, he goes through a folder that holds the 3,000 invitations to schools that he receives each year and chooses a classroom to visit. Sometimes, if it is near

Guelph, he'll just jump into his car and drop by for a visit, often without any warning. Most times the teachers and principals are so excited about his arrival that they stop everything they are doing and invite him in. Sometimes, though, his plan backfires, like the day that he dropped in unannounced to South Public School in Simcoe, Ontario, only to discover that all the students were away on a field trip to the Norfolk County Fair. The secretary was very excited to see him but no one else was around so he had to drive back home.

When his school visits are a long way from his home, they must be much better planned because he needs to find a place to stay and doesn't want to arrive at an empty school. On those trips, he usually spends a day visiting classrooms and telling stories. Then he asks some local students to take him on a tour of the community so he can learn what kids think about the

place where they live. Robert never stays in hotels during his school tours; he prefers to stay with families, although he spends as little time as possible with the parents. Instead, he prefers to hang out with kids, checking out their toys, school work, and posters, and talking to them about what THEY think is important. He spends a lot of time listening, occasionally making up brand new stories about them after he hears something interesting. When the kids have gone to bed and he has to visit with the adults, he often gets very shy and quiet and has nothing to say, even though he was loud and funny all evening with their children.

All of this is very unusual behavior because visiting authors usually stay in hotels and hang out with teachers at the end of a school day. But Robert is not a typical author, especially because he doesn't

Lighthouse

At the end of a performance in Antigonish, NS in 1993, Robert was given a drawing of a lighthouse by eight-year-old Sarah Gillis and was immediately inspired to create a story about it.

Lighthouse: A Story of Remembrance tells of a young girl who insists her father fulfill a family tradition of visiting the local lighthouse in the middle of the night.

Robert gathered photographs of Sarah and the lighthouse so that the illustrator, Janet Wilson, could use them as models. When the book was published in 2003, 10 years after Sarah drew her picture, it included Sarah's original drawing on the first page.

charge any money for his visits. Most authors will charge between $500 and $1,000 a day, but of course, most authors are not millionaires who can afford to fly around Canada and the United States dropping in on strangers. Robert makes enough money from his books that he can afford to do things his way—and pay all his own bills.

One school visit that Robert will never forget was to St. Patrick Catholic School in Cobalt, Ontario where he met Jackie Livingston: one teacher who would not take "no" for an answer.

In 1998, the Heinz spaghetti company sponsored a Robert Munsch Zoodle contest for all schools across Canada. Students could send in Zoodle labels that their class had collected for a chance to win a free lunch with Robert Munsch. The students in Andrew Livingston's grade four class in Cobalt, a small mining town in northeastern Ontario, went crazy, thinking that if they ate hundreds of cans of Zoodles pasta they would win for sure. Their teacher, Jackie Livingston (who happened to be Andrew's mother), had already written to Robert Munsch a year earlier asking him to visit but he couldn't. So she encouraged her class to eat Zoodles morning, noon, and night—even for birthday parties. Despite sending in hundreds of entries, they didn't win.

Still, Mrs. Livingston did not give up. She wanted her son Andrew to meet Robert so badly that she had her class produce a book describing their Zoodle adventure—but he still didn't come. Instead, the Heinz Company sent them two cases of Zoodles. They were so sick of Zoodles by that point that they donated the forty-eight cans of pasta to the local food bank.

A couple of years later, she had her class send another book, this time outlining all the ways that he could travel north to Cobalt—including riding on a reindeer. Mrs. Livingston wrote a letter explaining that her son would be in high school the following year and she needed Robert to visit the elementary before he graduated. Robert jokes that he was so afraid she would send lumberjacks to cut down the trees in his yard that he agreed to fly up and spend a day at her school.

In 2002, Robert flew to the nearest airport and Mrs. Livingston took Andrew to pick him up. She was so excited that she gave Robert a big hug, even though she didn't know him. Andrew was very embarrassed and told the author how his mother was constantly doing things that humiliated him. Sitting in the back seat for the long drive, Robert made up a story about Andrew and his mother called "I'm So Embarrassed." The kids thought it was funny—although Mrs. Livingston felt it was an exaggeration.

As usual, Robert had a great visit with every class in the school and then flew home the next day. When he got home, he liked the new story so much that he typed it up right away and sent a copy to Andrew as a souvenir. Then he added it to his file of stories-in-progress and started testing it out at other schools. Two years later, his publisher agreed to use it in a new book, so Robert asked Mrs. Livingston for pictures of Cobalt—and of herself, Andrew, and Taylor Gordon, a schoolmate whose name also made it into the story. All the photos were passed on to Michael Martchenko, the illustrator who has provided pictures for most of Robert's funny books since 1980, so that he could create pictures that looked like the people and places Robert had seen during his visit.

Finally, in 2005, seven years after the failed Zoodle contest, Robert sent Andrew a copy of the book that featured him, his embarrassing mother, and the little town of Cobalt. Mrs. Livingston was very excited about the book and even more excited about the news that Robert was going to return to Cobalt for four days so that that the whole town could celebrate. Later that winter, Robert was given celebrity treatment. A chili dinner was held at Andrew's high school and a local bookstore organized a book party so that hundreds of people could get *I'm So Embarrassed!* signed by both the author and Andrew.

During his visit to Cobalt, Robert stayed with the Livingston family. Andrew slept on a couch in the basement and gave Robert his comfortable bedroom. Having seen Robert tell stories a few years before, Andrew expected his guest to be wild and crazy but found him to be pretty "laid back." At the Saturday morning book signing, Andrew quickly noticed that there were two sides to the author. Whenever kids were around for autographs, "Robert acted really crazy," recalls Andrew. "But when he was surrounded by adults, he was serious."

Unfortunately, the night before the book signing, when Andrew and Robert were competing in a curling bonspiel, the teenager slipped on the ice and hurt his arm. At the bookstore the next morning, he signed a lot of books but finally said that his arm hurt so much that he had to give up. Robert sent him home to have a rest and, a few hours later, a doctor discovered that Andrew had been autographing books with a broken arm!

Chapter Eight

"Mr. Munsch— On Stage, Please!"

A man of a hundred faces, Robert uses his face and his hands to bring his stories to life during a performance in Pictou, Nova Scotia.

obert knows that he will never be able to see all the teachers and students who invite him for school visits—even though he drops in on about fifty schools annually. So for four weeks a year, he goes on tour with a professional production company that sells up to 20,000 tickets a week. The shows travel all across Canada and sometimes to the United States but are much different than Robert's classroom visits. Because the big audiences pay to hear his famous books and would not be happy listening to new unpolished stories that are not always perfect, Robert tells the stories from his collection of published books. When Robert visits for free, he does what he wants; when an audience pays him thousands of dollars a performance, he does what they want.

His largest show ever was in an arena in Red Deer, Alberta—15,000 people crowded in to see him; but it was a disaster because it was hard to hear him or see him. These days, his touring performances are much better organized.

In January 2007, Robert performed three shows in Ottawa's Centrepoint Theatre, entertaining about 900 children and parents at each show. Half of the audience consisted of parents and grandparents, and the other half were children, mainly under seven years of age. Most of the little girls wore their best dresses and a few wore little princess tiaras, hoping to hear *The Paper Bag Princess*. When Robert began *Love You Forever*, hundreds of people rocked imaginary babies back and forth in their arms as he sang the theme song in his raspy voice.

Before each show, Robert paces back and forth anxiously backstage, walking in circles and worrying about which story to tell first. He practices his stories in his head until he becomes "an agitated mess." Once he decides on his first story, he will peer cautiously out at the audience looking for kids who will fit into his act— perhaps searching for girls with ponytails who might come up on stage if he tells his ponytail story. Usually when he steps out on stage, he only knows what his first couple of stories will be and chooses the rest depending on the mood of the crowd.

He doesn't get all dressed up, preferring simple short sleeve shirts, blue jeans, and hiking boots. The stage has a microphone and two stools, one for him and the other for a kid he will call up before each story. He picks the children out of the audience, asking for volunteers. "I want a noisy kid," he says for one. "Who has a ponytail?" he asks for another. The young volunteers are excited and he rewards them by replacing each main character with the volunteer's name. A little boy named Logan stars in *I Have to Go*, even though it is Andrew who needs to pee all the time in the book. As a joke, Robert leans down and says, in a loud whisper, "Remember this is just a story."

Over the hour, Robert tells 14 stories. The audience chants along with the most popular parts and applauds enthusiastically after each one. Half way through the show, the youngest kids are getting squirmy, climbing on and off their parents' laps. A little girl named Sarah throws a tantrum near the end when she realizes that she is not going to be invited on stage. When the hour is up and his last story ends, Robert looks shyly out at the audience and simply says, "Thank you. Goodbye," and walks off the stage.

Chapter Nine

Family Man

Robert and his Munschkins, Andrew, Tyaa, and Julie (1985)

Back in 1980, Ann and Robert did not know how famous Robert Munsch the storyteller/author was going to become. In those days, despite the excitement surrounding the publication of his first three books, they were just an ordinary couple who wanted a houseful of children. When they knew that they couldn't have babies of their own, they decided to try adoption.

In 1980, Robert and Ann adopted a brand new baby boy named Andrew. Less than a year later, they added a five-and-a-half-year-old girl, Julie, to their family, giving Andrew an instant big sister. In 1985, three-month-old Tyaa joined them. Finally, they had the family they had dreamed about for years.

Having never written a book about his own childhood, Robert began to make up stories for—and about—his own children. Julie was already in kindergarten when she arrived and was begging for bedtime stories like Robert had heard from his own father in Etna. One of the first he created for her was *David's Father*, which he told to her every night for four months. She loved the story but kept making suggestions and asking for changes. She wanted a father who didn't look like his daughter (Julie is black and Robert is white). And she wanted a little girl who was afraid to go to school. Robert reworked the story for her every night and didn't share it with anyone else for a long time. But when he finally added it to his storytelling repertoire, kids loved it and so did his publisher.

As Andrew got older, Robert wrote a book about a boy's loose tooth for him (*Andrew's Loose Tooth*) and also used him in *I Have to Go. Purple, Green and Yellow*, about a girl who colors herself with markers, is dedicated to Tyaa. Julie also inspired *The Giant* (or *Waiting for the Thursday Boat*), a story about a giant who argues with God, who is a woman.

Growing up with a storytelling father named Robert Munsch sounds like a pretty exciting childhood, but when Tyaa and Andrew were young, their dad was not very well known as an author. They got to enjoy their very own private performances at story-time and loved to go out for Halloween with their parents. Ann would make fabulous costumes for them with some help from her husband. One year they cut holes in a garbage can so that Andrew could go out as a container of toxic sludge.

Generally, the first two children had pretty ordinary childhoods, although as more teachers around Guelph started reading Munsch books to their classes, they began to interrupt family shopping trips to share ideas with Robert about how schools could use his stories. The children would get bored and restless around the shopping cart while Robert listened politely.

Julie was about fourteen years old when *Love You Forever* first sold a million copies. That is when her parents decided to move from their small town-house to a bigger home. When the banker loaning them money found out how many books Robert was selling each year, he told them they could afford a $15 million mansion but Robert

A Hairy Story

Some of Robert's stories are based on his family, and others come from ideas sent to him from kids all around the world. But the idea for his book *Aaron's Hair* was inspired by a long-haired little boy named Aaron who attended the University of Guelph daycare centre. Robert wrote a story about Aaron's long uncontrollable hair running away. Fifteen years later, when the story was about to become a book, Robert tracked Aaron down to find him all grown up in Toronto, still fighting with his long hair–and playing in a rock band.

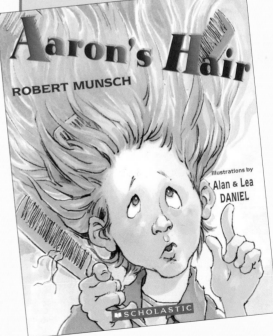

The Munsches on holiday at Dunns Falls, Jamaica.
From left, Robert, Ann, Andrew, Julie, and Tyaa

and Ann explained that they just wanted a regular house like everyone else.

Tyaa was one year old in 1986 when *Love You Forever* was published, so she was the only child in the family who grew up with a famous father, and occasionally she tried to take advantage of it. One summer when Robert and Ann asked her why she was always bringing friends home for lunch, they discovered that kids were paying $5 each to eat lunch with the famous Robert Munsch. Tyaa's first experiment with marketing ended immediately.

The Munsch kids, grown up. From left, Andrew, Julie, and Tyaa

These days, the Munsch children are grown up. Julie runs her own company in Toronto, planning special events for large companies. Andrew is an engineer (which is one of the jobs Mr. Munsch wanted for his son, Robert) and Tyaa, who has her own apartment in Guelph, is still undecided about her future but drops in to see her parents regularly.

With their own family grown up and their daycare days far behind them, Robert and Ann lead a quiet, comfortable life. But they are certainly not free of children. Each day the post office and their computer deliver letters and emails from children all across North America, reminding them that they are still in the business of caring for kids. And hardly a day goes by that Robert doesn't see something that inspires an idea that just might make a great story.

Chapter Ten

Happy Ending

Robert reads the day's email in the home office in his basement.

For people who know him, there are two Mr. Munsches. There is Robert Munsch, the storyteller with the crazy facial expressions and funny noises who tells wild stories just to make people laugh. And there is Bob Munsch, the quiet man next door who loves his family and his job but leads a peaceful, suburban life.

When he is at home, "Bob" gets up early every morning and takes his two dogs, Guinness, a large black poodle, and Winston, a Yorkshire terrier, for a long walk in the country and has a small breakfast before heading down to his basement office. There are no plaques or medals on the walls, although he has won a few. He was named to the Order of Canada in 2000, chosen the 78th most famous Canadian in history by CBC (hockey and donut legend Tim Horton was #59, John McCrae, author of the poem "In Flanders Fields" was #76), and became Guelph's Citizen of the Year for 2006.

His secretary, Sharon Bruder, handles the dozens, sometimes hundreds, of letters and emails he gets every day. She puts the interesting ones in neat piles for him to read and most of his fans get a reply, usually from Sharon (although Robert signs the letters and often tells her what to write).

Sometimes, a child will ask if he has a story about a particular subject—maybe on stars—and if he does he will send them a copy. "But," he adds, "it might not be a very good one so I do a rewrite and send it off.… I say I'm going to answer some mail from kids but it always ends up that I'm doing a story. I have trouble getting anything done."

Since he wrote down his first 10 stories to send out to publishers in 1978, Robert's story folder has grown a lot fatter; it has now been moved from the clutter on top of his desk to the desktop of his computer. He manages his story folder as if it were a garden, lovingly opening a few stories up each week to read them over and give them a little tweak—or a major rewrite.

Like all gardeners, Robert is anxious to share his crop, so he was disappointed several years ago when Annick decided to publish just one Munsch book each year instead of two. In 1997, he switched to Scholastic Publishing, a much larger company, which promised to release two books a year. That year he gave them almost one hundred stories to choose from and has since added another hundred. No publisher would be willing to publish so many books by the same author so Robert performs some of them for kids during his school visits so that they are not wasted.

Robert likes his life as a storyteller. Years ago, he earned a masters degree in anthropology, and now he gets to apply his expertise to the observation of children, pretend-ing they are a strange culture and that he has to figure out what they are doing. "I see them rolling down a hill and I say, 'What are they doing?'" Then he makes up a story about it. Maybe he misinterprets the situation on purpose,

Timeline

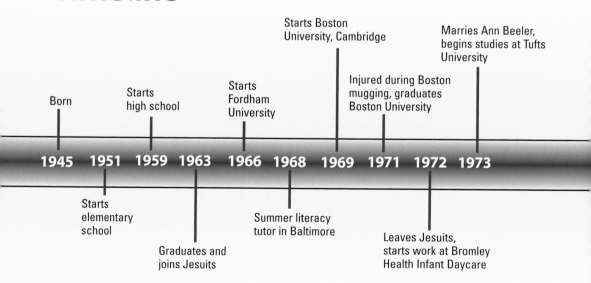

Starts Boston University, Cambridge

Marries Ann Beeler, begins studies at Tufts University

Starts high school

Starts Fordham University

Injured during Boston mugging, graduates Boston University

Born

1945 1951 1959 1963 1966 1968 1969 1971 1972 1973

Starts elementary school

Summer literacy tutor in Baltimore

Graduates and joins Jesuits

Leaves Jesuits, starts work at Bromley Health Infant Daycare or he exaggerates it—but that is usually how a funny story is born.

When kids hear a story, they say, "Oh yeah!" because they recognize themselves. Robert explains, "When I say, 'I HAVE TO GO PEEEEE…' the kids will nudge their fathers because that's real."

He knows he has created a good story when the audience spontaneously joins in and starts repeating phrases. That is when he knows they are hooked and that he has captured something special.

At schools, teachers and students will often ask for advice on writing.

"I tell them if they're making up stories to keep doing it.… To keep doing it because it's fun. And, you have to keep working on something until it's good."

And that is the secret of Robert Munsch's stories.

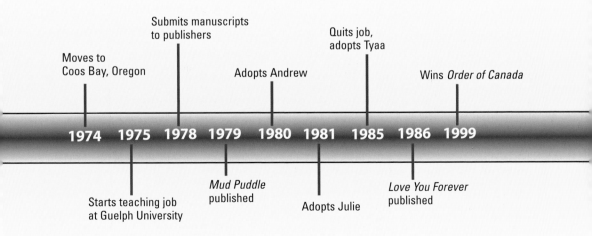

Submits manuscripts to publishers

Quits job, adopts Tyaa

Moves to Coos Bay, Oregon

Adopts Andrew

Wins *Order of Canada*

1974 1975 1978 1979 1980 1981 1985 1986 1999

Starts teaching job at Guelph University

Mud Puddle published

Adopts Julie

Love You Forever published

Index

Bibliography

1979	Mud Puddle
1979	The Dark
1980	The Paper Bag Princess
1981	Jonathan Cleaned Up– Then He Heard a Sound
1982	Murmel Murmel Murmel
1983	The Fire Station
1983	David's Father
1984	Millicent and the Wind
1985	Mortimer
1985	Thomas' Snowsuit
1986	The Boy in the Drawer
1986	50 Below Zero
1986	Love You Forever
1987	I Have To Go!
1988	Angela's Airplane
1988	A Promise is a Promise
1989	Giant (or Waiting for the Thursday Boat)
1989	Pigs!
1990	Something Good
1990	Good Families Don't
1991	Show and Tell
1992	Get Me Another One
1992	Purple, Green and Yellow
1993	Wait and See
1994	Where is Gah-Ning?
1995	Moira's Birthday
1995	From Far Away
1996	Stephanie's Ponytail
1997	Alligator Baby
1998	Get Out of Bed
1998	Andrew's Loose Tooth
1999	We Share EVERYTHING!
1999	Ribbon Rescue
2000	Aaron's Hair
2000	Mmm, Cookies
2001	Up, Up, Down
2001	Makeup Mess
2002	More Pies
2002	Playhouse
2003	Lighthouse
2003	Zoom
2004	Boo!
2004	Deep Snow
2004	Smelly Socks
2005	The Sandcastle Contest
2005	I'm So Embarrassed!
2006	No Clean Clothes
2007	Class Clown
2008	Just One Goal
2008	Look at Me!

Anthologies

1998	Munschworks, The First Munsch Collection
1999	Munschworks 2, The Second Munsch Treasury
2000	Munschworks 3, The Third Munsch Treasury
2001	Munschworks Grand Treasury
2002	Munschworks 4: The Fourth Munsch Treasury
2004	Munsch More!
2007	Much More Munsch!

Image Credits

All photographs courtesy of Robert Munsch from his personal collection with the following exceptions:

front and back cover photographs – courtesy of Scholastic Canada Ltd.

p. 9, 51, 49 – photos courtesy of Scholastic Canada Ltd.

p. 10, 64 – photos by Frank. B. Edwards

p. 38 – photo courtesy of University of Guelph

p. 42 – photo courtesy of Michael Martchenko

p. 11 – illustration by Michael Martchenko (*Up, Up, Down*), 2001. Courtesy of Scholastic Canada Ltd.

p. 15 – illustration by Michael Martchenko (*Thomas' Snowsuit*), 1985. Courtesy of Annick Press.

p. 42 – illustration by Michael Martchenko (*The Paper Bag Princess*), 1980. Courtesy of Annick Press.

p. 43 – illustration by Michael Martchenko (*The Paper Bag Princess: The Story Behind the Story*), 2005. Courtesy of Annick Press.

p. 45 – illustration by Sheila McGraw (*Love You Forever*), 1986. Courtesy of Firefly Books.

p. 48 – illustration by Anthony Lewis (*Love You Forever*). Courtesy of Firefly Books.

p. 52 – illustration by Sarah Gillis. Courtesy of Robert Munsch.

p. 55 – illustration by Michael Martchenko (*I'm So Embarrassed!*), 2005. Courtesy of Scholastic Canada Ltd.

p. 61 – illustration by Alan and Lea Daniel (*Aaron's Hair*), 2000. Courtesy of Scholastic Canada Ltd.

About the Author:

Frank B. Edwards has written 23 children's books and 4 non-fiction adult titles since he quit his job 20 years ago. Trained as a journalist, Frank worked initially as a magazine editor and feature writer at the Canadian Geographic, Harrowsmith, and Equinox before becoming a book publisher and editor. In 1986, he co-founded Bungalo Books with illustrator/author John Bianchi.

Frank writes for both adults and children, telling stories through web exhibits, museum programs, television scripts, and magazine articles, Besides writing books, he also works as an educational consultant. The father of three adult children, Frank lives beside a quiet lake in eastern Ontario.